# Married and No Sex Anymore

Published by
Luviri Press
P/Bag 201 Luwinga
Mzuzu 2
Malawi

ISBN      978-99960-66-24-5
eISBN     978-99960-66-25-2

Luviri Press is represented outside Malawi by:
African Books Collective Oxford (order@africanbookscollective.com)

www.luviripress.blogspot.com

www.africanbookscollective.com

Editorial assistance and cover: Hope Kapombe, Josephine Kawejere and Daniel Neumann

Printed in Malawi by Baptist Publication, P.O. Box 444, Lilongwe

# Married and no Sex anymore:
# Mbulu as a Pastoral Problem in Mzimba in Northern Malawi

Bonet Byton Kamwela

Luviri Press
Mzuzu
2020

# Table of Contents

# Dedication

This book is dedicated to both my late father Bishop Byton Anania Kamwela of African International Church (AIC), who died on 19<sup>th</sup> of December, 2006 and my mother Goodness Swila who continues to encourage me to work hard spiritually and physically. Dad, may your soul rest in peace, Mum continue the good job you started with Dad. May God bless you.

# Acknowledgements

I am very thankful to my dear and loving wife, Roselyne Mkwala and my children, Ambele, Tuntufye and Lughano for their support and great patience they rendered to me while I was writing this book. Thanks also to my brothers and sisters, especially; Hencewell, William, Tomas, Florence, Joy and Judith for supporting me in one way or another on this project.

I would also like to thank Gilbert P. Chima, session clerk of Kafukule CCAP and his wife NyaJere for the hospitality and accommodation rendered to me during my research. Thanks also to the following: Rev. B.R.C. Mwakasungula for accommodating me in his boy's quarters during my two years of study at Ekwendeni, Rev. Robin H. Quinn for all the assistance rendered to me during my stay in the boy's quarters, Rev Godwin Mdoka Chirambo, who had been my closest friend, also for helping me with some of my personal needs.

Special thanks to the late Rev Dr D.S. Mwakanandi, the former Principal of the College of Theology Ekwendeni, for his great encouragement he offered to me. May his soul rest in peace. I also don't forget Rev Debbie A. Chase who has great influence in my theological education and the support she gave to my family while at the college. Also thanks should go to Professor Klaus Fiedler, my supervisor during this research.

Finally, I want to express my deep appreciation to Revs. William Mtayisi Kalua, Chance K. Mwangomba and Edward Kamthuzi Ng'oma for helping me with computer skills, when I was writing this book.

# Introduction

Mzimba is situated in the northern part of Malawi. It is the largest district in the Northern Region. It is occupied by Ngoni and Tumbuka. In Mzimba many couples misunderstand each other on issues of sex when the woman reaches menopause. In this case, the woman refuses to have sex with her husband in fear of *mbulu*. This belief of *mbulu* is very common in Mzimba, mainly among the women who have reached this stage. They believe that sleeping with a man after menopause is dangerous because sperms will turn and grow into lizards (*mbulu*) in the stomach. They believe that un-used sperms come out during menstruation, but since the period is past, these sperms will remain in the womb and grow into living creatures causing the woman to swell the stomach and then later die. The refusal of sex after menopause causes many differences in a marriage and has become a challenge to many men who are sexually active.

# Chapter One

## *Mbulu* in the Traditional Culture of Mzimba

In any African society, there are traditions to follow. Although they are not written in books, they are passed from one generation to the other verbally or through watching from elders of the society. Not all the beliefs have proper reasons. Not at all! The younger generations are commanded to follow because it is the inheritance from their ancestors, ignoring them, the ancestors will be angry and consequences will follow. Because of this there is no question of why. Mzimba is not exceptional of these beliefs. In African Tradition Religion (ATR) the ancestors referred to as the living dead, controlling the everyday life of their living kin.

There are many beliefs people of Mzimba follow. My focus is the *mbulu* belief. *Mbulu* is a reptile known as lizard. This belief is followed by many women who have reached menopause. Traditionally, these women have passed the age of sex. So they are not supposed to sleep with their husbands or any man, because sperms will not find a fertile place to make a baby nor will they find the way out. Un-used sperms are believed to come out during menstruation. Because the woman can no longer be in monthly period, these sperms will not go out but remain in the womb and grow into *mbulu*. These *mbulu* will cause the woman's stomach to swell and lead to her death according to tradition.

Whenever couples enter into marriage, they are instructed many things such as how to live a good marriage. They are instructed some beliefs which are to be followed and others which are not to be followed. *Mbulu* belief is one of the traditions instructed to be followed in later days to a woman who enters into marriage. She is instructed by her aunts and old women. Whenever a woman reaches menopause, she begins to implement the instructions told to her during the early days of her marriage. Not all the things we do in our everyday life were taught at *mphara* or *nthanganene* (a house for boys or girls respectively) or in class at school. Neither are they are found in the Bible and the Quran which are guides to life for Christians and Muslims respectively. Some of these things we follow we just learn through watching or listening to friends.[1] Many women who missed instructions about *mbulu* belief during their marriage, just listen to stories from friends. *Mbulu* is an inherited belief from ancestors in Mzimba. Nobody can trace when it started and who started it.

## Mzimba District

Mzimba is one of the districts in the Northern Region of Malawi. It is also the largest in the country. In the north, it borders with Rumphi District. In the east it borders with Nkhata-Bay District. In the South it borders with Kasungu and in the West, it borders with Zambia.

Mzimba is referred to as Ngoniland. This clearly shows that it is occupied by the Ngoni and ruled by the Ngoni. The title of their ruler is Chief Mbelwa. The present Mbelwa is Mbelwa V. The Tumbuka are also dominating in the district. This is due to intermarriage. Because of immigration people from many others tribes such as the Ngonde, Ndali, Chewa, Yawo and many others are found in Mzimba.

---

[1] Int. Maggie Soko, church elder, Kafukule CCAP, (not real name), 6.1.2013.

# Cultural Beliefs on Mbulu

*Mbulu* belief is an old tradition in Mzimba. It is not known when and who started it. Many people have followed it and are still following it, although in some parts it has started to be abandoned. But still it is an outstanding belief in many parts of Mzimba. Some Christians too follow this tradition regardless of accepting Jesus as their personal Saviour. If not followed according to tradition, it is believed to cause many problems. Below I will try to explain some of the consequences of *mbulu* belief.

## *Chikhoso or Moto*

*Chikhoso* or *moto* is a disease believed to be caused by *mbulu*. This *chikhoso* or *moto* will affect the infants, old people and even domestic animals.

> "Nadi baliska, para agogo wali na mbulu ndipo wapakata mwana muchoko panji watawuzgana namuchekulu munyake panji wenda kuchibaya pa chikaya pakuwa chikhoso panji moto."[2]

To avoid this *chikhoso* or *moto,* an African doctor is invited to prepare medicine for all the members of the family, from the youngest to the oldest. He/she prepares the medicine in form of porridge and it is put in a *chihengo* (winnowing basket) so that every member of the family drinks the medicine from it. After taking the medicine the *chikhoso* or *moto* vanishes, the

---

[2] Int. Nyasulu, church elder, Kafukule CCAP (not real name), 27.2.2013. ("Indeed Rev. Sir, if an old woman is affected by *mbulu* and has carried a child or greeted an old person or walks around the kraal, that particular home is affected by *chikhoso* or *moto*. Even cattle in the kraal catch the disease.")

infants, the old people and the animals become safe from the disease.

> "Three times in my life I have drunk this medicine from the *chihengo* because of *mbulu* beliefs. Three women were affected by *mbulu* in our family at different times. In each case the known African doctor for this particular medicine was invited for his duty. Every member of the family drank the medicine from the winnowing basket."[3]

When the head of the family called for this meeting every member of the family attended. Ignoring the call for such a meeting was like signing your death warrant. In all the three cases the compound of the village was full to capacity.[4]

## Deaths

The other way *chikhoso* or *moto* comes into the family is when the husband whose wife has reached menopause is sleeping with other women. This practice is believed to bring *chikhoso* or *moto* into the family. This *chikhoso* or *moto* will bring about the death of infants, old people and animals in the family. To avoid this *chikhoso* or *moto* in the family, the African doctor puts the medicine on the fire place or in the pot of drinking water and throws some in the kraal. Every member of the family is to take fire from there to make his/her own, and must also drink from the pot with medicine. In so doing deaths will be avoided for both people and animals. This is a tradition, whenever such incident has happened, the African doctor is invited for his duties.

---

[3] Int. Adams, retired teacher and church elder, CCAP (not real name), 27.2.2013.
[4] Ibid.

## Herbs for the Affected Woman

According to African tradition every disease is curable because it has its own medicine. *Mbulu* too is believed to have medicine which is said to be very effective at an early stage. When a woman is affected by *mbulu*, her stomach swells, the arteries along the neck protrude and breathing becomes difficult. After inviting the African doctor, the woman is given some medicine. I saw a woman who was given medicine at an early stage, she purged heavily and became well.[5] Indeed there is that chance of living, if the medicine is given in time. In the case of giving the medicine too late, terrible things happen.

> "I cannot remember the year, but I was already married when one of the old women in our village was affected by *mbulu*. Her stomach was almost transparent and bursting."[6]

She described the disease in great details. Legs were swollen as if she was affected with elephantiasis. When she was given medicine, living creatures came out through the vagina. The doctor sprinkled them with some herbs and then killed them and burned them.[7] In some cases after these living creatures come out, the woman dies. In this case the dead body is taken out for burial, the living creatures are killed by the herbalist, and the house is broken and burnt.

The belief of breaking the house in Ngoniland is not only for those who have died of *mbulu*, even a house of any widow or widower is broken soon after her or his burial. This practice is followed in many parts of Mzimba, mainly when the house is not iron sheet roofed. The breaking of the house of a dead old

---

[5] Int. NyaChavula, cook at Theological College, Ekwendeni, 12.2.2013.
[6] Int. *Gogo* Mfipa (not real name), 27.2.2013.
[7] Ibid.

person symbolizes that the spirits of that person are chased away. Even her belongings are burnt in fear of *mbulu*. The dead body is not surrounded by many young women in fear of the disease. If the house is not burnt the spirit of the dead person will still live in that house. In this case of *mbulu*, there is a belief that any woman who can occupy that house the spirits of the dead will enter her and she too will one day be affected with *mbulu*.

In any African society herbs are very important. Although many missionaries have tried to discourage the use of herbs they are still in use. Many Africans who claim to be Christians, use herbs in one way or another. At one time when I was trying to discourage the use of herbs in one of my parishes, one prominent church elder said,

> "Moderator Sir, you do not cease to be an African if you are converted to Christianity. An African will remain an African even if he is a committed Christian. So using herbs is not a sin."[8]

Because of this some committed Christians are also African doctors.[9]

## Sex with Young Men

Some women are more sexually active than men. These women have problems when their husbands die due to their old age, also when they reach menopause. They cannot satisfy themselves, when they sleep with old men, because of this they

---

[8]    Int. Mhango (not real name), 10.9.2012.

[9]    For a thesis that explores this phenomenon, see Chimwemwe Harawa-Katumbi, The Interaction between Christianity and Traditional Medicine in the Livingstonia Synod, MA, University of Malawi, 2003.

look for young men who are strong and can satisfy them. Since these young men are strong, traditionally it is believed that sperms of young men penetrate into the womb. Since they cannot come out or find eggs, they grow into *mbulu*.

> "After the death of my father, my step mother started sleeping with young men; as a result she was affected with *mbulu*, since she had already passed the age of sex according to tradition."[10]

Nyauhango (not real name) was the one caring for her step mother. She carried her to the hospital, after some treatment she started to be okay and she was discharged. At home the disease started again and she died. During her death she was bleeding from her mouth and nose. There were some movements on her stomach. Some people thought she had come back to life. Elders of the village whispered that the *mbulu* were struggling to come out which caused the movements of her stomach and the bleeding. There was blood everywhere in the room where she was laid.[11] Many people were afraid to enter the room where the dead body was laid.

## How *Mbulu* Belief is followed in Mzimba

*Mbulu* tradition is still followed in many parts of Mzimba, although some people, because of education and Christianity, have abandoned it as an old tradition. But the majority of people still follow it in different ways. This tradition is not followed openly but secretly. It is only the husband and the wife who know this.

---

[10]  Int. Nyauhango, (not real name), 12.9. 2012.
[11]  Ibid.

## Sleeping with Grandchildren in the same Room

Many old couples in the villages are cared for by their grandchildren. Traditionally, when the father or the mother gets old, the son or daughter sends a child to care for them. In this case, when a woman stops menstruation, she invites her grandchild to her bedroom. During sleeping time, the grandchild either sleeps between them or sleeps with her grandmother on her bed. In so doing, even if the old man had interest in his wife, he cannot do anything in the presence of the grandchild. The grandchild is ignorant of what is happening. He/she feels is loved by both. For a young child sleeping with the grandparents is a prestige. Grandparents are very kind to their grandchildren. Many children in the villages like to go to live with their grandparents.

## Separation of Rooms

Men are created in such a way that they can be attracted to a woman in many ways. A man is attracted to a woman just by looking at her. This becomes a problem to the husband if they can no longer have sex together and yet they sleep in one room. To avoid such problems the two agree to separate the rooms. Sometimes the woman changes the room in fear of being raped by her husband; in this case there is no agreement. By doing that *mbulu* belief is being followed since the two never sleep together anymore as husband and wife. Therefore, the woman cannot get *mbulu* because they don't have sex together. Some men understand this belief of separation for the health of their wives while others do not because their sexual passions are too strong.

## Medication

There are many ways of killing a rat. When the wife has reached menopause but they do not want to stop conjugal sex, some couples look for medicine. There are different types of medicines and different ways of using them according to tradition; some medicine is taken by the woman before sex, so that when sperms enter the womb, they meet the medicine and it is believed that they die. So every time they are to have sex the woman takes a cup of medicine. In the past there was no child spacing as we have it today at any hospital.

> "We used this method until the child was weaned between two to three years. Do you think we were just looking at each other as brothers and sisters until the child was weaned? Until today we still enjoy sex using this method."[12]

Sometimes it is the man who chews a small root and swallows the saliva whenever they play sex. In this case the sperms are believed to be weakened so that they cannot produce anything even if they may enter the womb. This method also helps them during child spacing. Many young boys are believed to use this medicine when they play sex with their girlfriends. In this way it is believed that a girl cannot get pregnant. This practice of someone swallowing medicine for another person as a preventive way is not a strange thing in Mzimba. When someone has been bitten by a snake called *nkhomi,* she or he is healed in this way. Someone who is not bitten sits on the bitten one and drinks medicine on behalf of the bitten one and he/she is healed.

Another kind of medicine is in form of a string made into two throngs with knots within it. When the couple is to have sex,

---

12    Int. NyaGondwe, (not real name), 19.9.2012.

the woman ties the string around her waist. According to tradition this will prevent the sperms from entering the womb, therefore a woman cannot get *mbulu* or get pregnant.

> "When my husband was alive, I used to put on beads. This was not only for attraction for his sexual desire but the string holding the beads was medicine. My husband died when I was 69, but we had no sex problems."[13]

Knots in the strings are numbers of years a woman can put it on without getting pregnant. This shows that a string is to be renewed when the years have passed according to the number of knots. If the string is not renewed, the woman might get the *mbulu* or might get pregnant.

Wearing of things as protective mechanism is very common in Mzimba. A chief puts on a ring on his arm as a symbol of chieftainship as well as protective material. When someone is having neck pains, he/she puts on a string around the neck. This string is believed to be medicine for the neck. Infants are dressed with strings around their necks, waists, hands and legs. All these strings are defensive mechanism against spirits and other diseases that can attack the chief and the children respectively.

When someone is bitten by a snake or a scorpion, a string is tied above the bitten part so that the poison should not spread in the whole body. It is believed that the string will prevent the spreading of the poison. So using strings as a defensive mechanism against *mbulu* is not a strange thing to them. Even during child spacing some use the same strings by putting them around the waist when they play sex preventing the sperms from entering the womb.

---

[13] Int. Gogo Nyausowoya (not real name), 26.1.2013.

Another medicine is put under the bed in an earthen pot. When the couple wants to have sex, this pot is covered with its lid. In so doing, sperms do not enter the womb according to tradition. By covering the pot, they believe they are blocking the way of sperms to enter the womb. But if the pot is not covered, it is believed that the woman is likely to have *mbulu,* since sperms will enter the womb because the way is open.

Africans believe that medicine can work anywhere it is placed for instance, when someone wants to trap thieves in his garden, he/she just places the medicine in the garden. So anyone coming into the garden without the owner's permission is trapped.

## Ejaculating Outside

A man is relieved from sexual passion soon after ejaculation. Since the wife is afraid of un-used sperms because of her age, the two agree that they should continue with sex but the man should ejaculate outside. The man agrees for the sake of the health of his wife. During sex, when the man is about to ejaculate, he moves up, and as a result he ejaculates outside. In some cases the man becomes too weak to move himself up. In this case the wife senses that the husband is about to finish his duty, she just pushes him aside gently while still holding him tight to herself and then he ejaculates outside.

> "We still have that pleasure of sex through this system. Because of age we don't do it as frequently as we used to do. I am now 65 but I still have that passion once in a while."[14]

---

[14] Int. NyaMwale (not real name), 2.9.2012.

Another way of ejaculating outside is that the man does not enter his wife. He just places his penis between her thighs near the vagina and the wife moves up and down slowly by slowly, in the course of doing that the man feels very comfortable as if he has entered her, he then ejaculates.

> "Ise tawanakazi pakati pamalundi ghithu pafupi nacholi tikuthukila chomene, pala mwanalumi wawika khuli yake wakukhizga mtima ngati para tagonana."[15]

Also the man is relieved of his sexual passion just by his wife touching the end of his penis softly after love play. This makes him feel very comfortable as if he is playing sex, he then ejaculates. In so doing the man is relieved of his passion and the woman is protected from being affected with *mbulu*.

## Sleeping with Clothes on

With time tradition changes, the way of living also changes. These changes come in because of copying from other traditions. In the past women could not put on *belemuda* (big shorts trousers), but nowadays many women put on these big shorts under their normal dressing. When a woman realizes she has reached menopause, she uses *a belemuda* as a sleeping gown. This has been a routine for many women, many men have complained about their wives sleeping with clothes on, mainly the *belemuda*. This has caused many men to lose interest and trust in their wives.[16] This is not just a sleeping gown but a defensive mechanism against the husband in fear

---

[15] Int. NyaNkhambule, (not real name) "Between the thighs of a woman near the vagina it is warm and when the man places his penis there he feels comfortable as if playing sex."

[16] Int. Eunice Phiri, Njuyu Presbytery Women Coordinator, 9.9.2012.

of being raped and be affected with *mbulu*. These *belemuda* cannot be undressed easily by the husbands.

## The Use of Condoms

Some families who are still holding the belief of *mbulu* but are a bit educated use condoms.

> "I am now 73 and my wife is 66, we have not separated as others do, we still have sex but use condoms, although my wife has much less interest in sex nowadays than she used to have. All the time, it is me who starts but she never refuses although she says she does not enjoy it as she used to do. Sometimes she says she feels pain when we play sex."[17]

The use of condoms has been received negatively by some couples. Some feel it is unhealthy to use condoms. Other women feel it can remain in the vagina; still some feel condoms are for prostitutes.

> "As old as I am, using condoms, why? How will people think of me? These condoms are for young ones and prostitutes, after all I will still not feel anything. It is better for me to stay without sex than using condoms.[18]

## Mitala (Polygamy)

*Mitala* means that a man has more than one wife at a time. When the wife reaches menopause, she may initiate her husband to marry a second wife who will relieve her from sexual matters. According to tradition the wife is to be involved in finding the second wife. The second wife is from the wife's

---

[17]   Int. Mhango, retired teacher (not real name), 24.11.2012.
[18]   Int. NyaMoyo, (not real name), 26.11.2012.

relatives so that the man should continue to support the same family. If he marries from another family the support will not continue to the family of the first wife, the attention will be on the new wife's family.[19] The arrival of the second wife is a blessing to both the man and the first wife. The man is blessed in the sense that there is someone strong where he can relieve himself, while the first wife is blessed because she is now free from the dangers of *mbulu*. Not all polygamists are married for the sake of *mbulu,* not at all. Some men entered into polygamy because of other reasons known to them.

## Why *Mbulu* Belief is followed in Mzimba

Each tribe has its own traditional beliefs. These beliefs are inherited from one generation to another from the ancestors. They need to be followed systematically as long as someone lives. Failure to follow these beliefs will draw punishment from the living dead, the originators of the tradition. In this case *mbulu* belief is to be followed well to avoid some of these consequences meted out by the forefathers.

### To Avoid Chikhoso or Moto

*Chikhoso* or *moto* is a disease caused by not following *mbulu* belief. This disease will affect infants, old people and domestic animals. The infants and the old people develop a cough and their bodies are always warm. Animals' hairs stand up. The animals look like feeling cold. Both people and animals have no appetite to eat. If the tradition is not followed well, this disease will not end in that particular family. To avoid this disease the belief is to be followed very well in every family according to

---

[19]   Int. NyaChavula, Cook, Theological College, Ekwendeni, 12.2.2013.

the tradition. If *chikhoso or moto* is not attended to quickly, it will lead to poor health of people and livestock.

## To Avoid Death

Any disease, if not well cured, leads to death. Many people have died because of *mbulu* in different ways, according to tradition. Firstly, the affected; if someone affected is not treated quickly, she loses her life. To avoid deaths of the affected women, the tradition is to be followed seriously.

Secondly, there are the deaths of infants and old people in the society who have been carried or greeted by the affected woman. They do not live long if medicine is not given in time. It is very difficult for the affected to come into the open to say she has *mbulu*. Since grandchildren are being cared for by their grandparents, mainly when their parents are in the fields, infants are affected very easily and die easily. Traditionally deaths of an infant and an old person are often associated with *mbulu* belief in Mzimba.

Thirdly are the deaths of domestic animals. If this belief is not taken seriously, even animals die.

> "I am speaking this from what I saw, many young children and animals died because my own grandmother was affected with *mbulu*. She was discovered by an African doctor, but after many problems in the society. When she was given some medicine, she died on the spot. After burial her house was broken and burnt. That marked the end of deaths of infants and animals in the society."[20]

---

[20] Int. Nkhoswe (not real name), 26.2.2013.

If the doctor has not identified quickly the culprit, those with infants and old women go away of that home and stay with relatives somewhere for protection from the disease. Because of all these problems, which are believed to have been caused by *mbulu,* it is advisable that this tradition should be followed accordingly.

According to African tradition, death of a person is always associated with a living person or the living dead. When a person dies, the question is who has killed him/her? Or what have we wronged the living dead with? This is the reason why, when a baby or an old person dies, it is associated with *mbulu.*

## Avoid Shaming the Society

Traditionally there are some diseases which bring shame to the society as well as to the affected. When a person has died with a shameful disease during the burial it is never said that he/she has died of such disease. In this case the affected will be ashamed in the sense that people will laugh at her. She will be regarded as a prostitute, a lover of men. The society is ashamed because the disease brings disgrace to the living as well as to the living dead. The living dead being the founders of the tradition are angry with such situations and might punish the society with a plague. To avoid this behaviour shameful to the society as well as to the living dead, this tradition must be followed according to tradition.

When HIV/AIDS was just discovered in Malawi people who were affected could not come into the open. This made many young people to lose their lives. This was because many people thought it was a shameful disease. At present people who are affected come out in the open because HIV/AIDS is now just like any other disease.

# Mbulu and Biology

Biologists have studied how the human body works from the womb until a person dies. The body works differently at different stages. The bodies of male and female are made different and work differently. There are many ways how the body of a woman works after reaching menopause. Menopause results from a decline in the function of her ovaries, two organs that produce the egg cell and hormones needed for reproduction.[21] *This shows that to a woman who has reached menopause, even if she has sex, nothing can happen in her womb because she does not produce eggs which could be fertilized.* The sperms will die a natural death because there is no suitable environment for them. In this case, sex after menopause is recommended at the hospital because nothing evil can happen, different from what traditionalists think.

Secondly there is no suitable passage for sperms to travel. Sperms travel in fluids to enter the womb. But in this case, they cannot travel into the womb because it is only the man who produces fluids; the woman is dry since her body can no longer produce these fluids.[22] For sperms to travel into the womb a woman must produce fluids during sex because fluids of a woman are the pathway of sperms to go into the womb. With the absence of fluids from the woman there is no way sperms can enter the womb.[23] This technology of sperms travelling in fluids is not known by the local man. It is only those who have studied Biology who know this. A local person thinks sperms enter the womb any time couples play sex. When the woman reaches menopause, her cervix closes with some substances

---

[21] *World Book 2001, Volume 13,* Chicago: World Book Inc., 2001, p. 402.

[22] Int. Mrs Kawelama, Matron, Ekwendeni Mission Hospital, 13.2.2013.

[23] Ibid.

like mucus.[24] This clearly shows that there is no way a sperm can enter the womb when a woman has reached menopause because the way is blocked by these substances. The enjoyment of sex does not change because the woman has reached menopause.

> "Reverend Sir, there is no such thing as *mbulu* in Biology. This is just a belief of which I too hear. Here at the hospital women are taught that there is no such thing, therefore they are encouraged to have sex even when they reach menopause because there is no effect."[25]

---

[24] Int. Mary Mhango, Nurse, Enukweni Health Centre, 2.9.2012.
[25] Int. Mrs Kawelama, Matron, Ekwendeni Mission Hospital, 13.2.2013.

# Chapter Two

## *Mbulu* as a Pastoral Problem

Mzimba is occupied by many Christians in particular members of the CCAP Synod of Livingstonia, the Roman Catholics, the Seventh Day and many other independent churches. These Christians have not forsaken some of their traditional beliefs for Christianity. One among them is *mbulu* belief. It is deeply rooted in Mzimba. When I ministered in Mzimba I faced many problems in connection with the belief during my pastoral work.

ATR is deeply rooted in Mzimba that even committed Christians practice it in one way or another. Just to cite a few examples, when a person dies, it is one of the elders of the village who knocks at the gate of the grave when they go early in the morning to dig the grave.

> "Odi, odi, tabana binu tafika kuti tizagwireko ntchito ku muzi kuno. Muzukulu winu ndiyo wafwa ndipo tiza pakunozga malo ghakuti wapumulepo kuno kumuzi."[26]

There are many other beliefs which are followed by many men who are sexually active.

## Problems Caused by *Mbulu* Belief in Marriages

There are many problems caused by *mbulu* belief. These problems have affected many marriages in Mzimba. Some

---

[26] "Knock, knock, we your children have come here to do some work. Your grand child is coming to join you here, so we have come to prepare a resting place for him/her."

marriages have even come to an end. In some cases, serving God has become a problem because of *mbulu* belief.

## Mitala (Polygamy)

There are many reasons why men practice *mitala* in Mzimba. One among them is *mbulu* belief. In this case, when the wife has passed the age of sex according to tradition, and if her husband cannot control himself, his wife proposes for him to take a second wife. The second wife should be a young and energetic woman who will relieve the husband of his sexual passions. This will save the first wife from contracting *mbulu*. It is the duty of the first wife to look for her own relative who will be the second wife. She can be her own sister, the daughter of her brother or any other close relative. This second wife, if she is a relative of the first wife, is called *mbiligha*. If there is no suitable woman from the wife's relatives, the husband is given the chance to look for himself from anywhere. Sometimes he is assisted by the wife.

The first wife is very happy when the second wife comes into the compound because she feels she is now free from the danger of *mbulu*. She is also relieved from other jobs like cooking and drawing water, just to mention few. Although the first wife is happy with the coming of the second wife, internally she realizes that her marriage will be affected in one way or another because her husband will not share the same love equally. He will give more attention to the second wife. But for the sake of her life she welcomes the problem with happiness.

According to CCAP Synod of Livingstonia, this man and the second wife must be suspended if they were full members of the church. This is because polygamous marriage is against the tradition and teaching of the church. These two suspended members will be denied some privileges such as partaking in Holy Communion, preaching, singing in a choir, to be elected to any position and many more. Because of this they will no longer be active members of the church. This becomes a pastoral problem. This problem affects even the children born from that marriage. Children too will not be baptized during their infancy. They have to wait until they start Sunday school and be baptized during adult baptism.

## Chibwezi (Vibwezi)

These are relationships between a man and a woman outside marriage or between a man and a woman who are not officially married. *Mbulu* belief is one of the contributing factors to *Vibwezi* in marriages. This practice of *Vibwezi* is common to many men who are still sexually active and whose wives have reached menopause. "This is the only alternative. I can't divorce my dear wife at this stage and marry another one. After all I just meet my *chibwezi* once in a while."[27] *The vibwezi* relationships shake many marriages because the man concentrates more on the *chibwezi* than on his real wife. This makes the marriage relationship sour. "My husband must be suspended because he has *chibwezi*."[28] When this family was visited the husband complained about the behaviour of the wife. The wife too complained with the movements of the husband. This becomes a pastoral problem until the husband disclosed that he really had *chibwezi* because his wife does not allow him sex because of her age. The practice of *vibwezi* indeed affects many marriages.

---

[27] Int. Mwale (not real name), 6.9.2012.
[28] Int. NyaBanda (not real name), 6.9.2012.

## Rape Cases of Granddaughters

Traditionally, grandfathers call their granddaughters their wives and grandmothers call their grandsons their husbands. According to tradition, when sons and daughters grow up, they are not allowed to enter into their parents' bedroom, while grandchildren are allowed to enter the bedroom of their grandparents. When the husband fails to convince his wife about conjugal issues when she has reached menopause, he looks for an alternative where to relieve himself. A granddaughter is the nearest alternative. When I was 13 years, I was raped by my grandfather.

> "He sent me to get his snuff in his bedroom which he said was under the mat. When I was still looking for it, he followed and closed the door,"[29]

explained a 63 years old woman. Since she was used to entering the room she just thought nothing about such kind of thing. She had never had sex with anybody, so she knew nothing about sex.

> "I was putting on my *chilundu* around my waist, so I was half naked and my breasts had just started to grow. He undressed and forced me to lie on the mat and placed his thing on my private part. When I shouted out for help because of pain he ran away. I was bleeding and dirty on my private part."[30]

Although many young girls have been raped in many ways by different men, *mbulu* belief has also contributed to some rape cases in Mzimba.

---

[29]  Int. NyaGondwe (not real name), 10.9.2012.
[30]  Ibid.

## *Separation of Rooms*

In Mzimba many grandparents live with their grandchildren. When the woman knows that she is through with her menstruation, they separate rooms with her husbands. She put up with the grandchildren while the husband is alone in his room. In some cases the husband puts up in the kitchen while the wife and the grandchildren put up in the main house. This separation system is a major problem in Mzimba. This type of living has caused many problems in marriages. A man is not cared for at all. A wife is afraid to enter into her husband's room in fear of being raped and be affected with *mbulu.* This separation system gives a chance to a man who has *chibwezi* to go and spend a night at her place without the wife noticing him. As a pastor of CCAP Synod of Livingstonia, who had worked in Mzimba for some good years I have seen this problem of *mbulu* belief with my naked eyes.

> "I have said this to you because you are my spiritual father. I love my wife very much. During wedding vows we promised to be united till death separates us. But my wife does not love me; she never sweeps and smears my room. I live as if not married because *mbulu* has separated us,"[31]

said a 75 years old man bursting into tears. He had never told anyone his marriage problem but it has been there for ten years. This is really a pastoral problem in the church in Mzimba.

The other problem is during sickness. Since they have separated the rooms, if the wife is sick, she is being cared by the grandchildren because they sleep together. But if it is the husband it becomes a problem. This has led to many unnoticed deaths, especially of men.

---

[31]   Int. Zakeyo (not real name), 22.10.2012.

"My brother's death was discovered after two days by his grandchild since his wife never entered his room after reaching menopause. It was a very painful death. His wife was chased; she did not attend the burial of her husband."[32]

## Breaking of Marriage

Denying sex to a husband who is sexually active is like punishing him.

"When I was not married, I was missing one thing, which I expected my wife to do for me the rest of my life as our wedding vows had said."[33]

When they had stayed in marriage for 34 years his wife reached menopause and started denying him sex in fear of *mbulu*. This was the beginning of the breaking of their marriage. There was no peace in the house; quarrels and fighting were the talk of the day. At last the man decided to break this marriage and marry another woman who would fulfil his sexual desires. According to tradition, "Mwanakazi wakugota mwanalume wakugotchara."[34]

The other duty of a wife in marriage is to warm the bed of the husband. In this case if the two have separated the bed will not be warmed. This is indeed true. Women are warmer than men. During the cold months of the year, a man finds refuge from the wife. Remember the story of King David when he was old, he was given a girl to warm his bed (1 King 1:2). A wife is more important in marriage to her husband in her old age as in her youth stage. Men and women are created differently. In my understanding women have heaters in their bodies so they are warmer than

---

[32] Int. Saka (not real name), 22.10.2012.

[33] Int. Soko (not real name), 19.10. 2012.

[34] ("A woman gets old while a man does not.") Int. Agness Thawi, Ekwendeni Presbytery Women Coordinator, Ekwendeni, 3.9.2012.

men. So during cold days a husband depends on his wife. During the night they cling to each other for warmth or a husband sleeps in front of his wife. A wife does not only provide sex to her husband but to help each in all times.

## Denial of Resources

In Mzimba, the husband is the owner of everything in the family. A wife has very little say on the belongings of the family. Since the woman has started denying sex to her husband because of her age according to tradition, the wife becomes an enemy. The husband begins to deny some resources to his wife as a punishment. This problem affects the whole family in the sense that denial of money for relish to the wife will result in the whole family missing the meal. *Mbulu* belief becomes the centre of this problem in the family. In the same way the wife cannot give her money to her husband. So denying each other resources between the husband and the wife becomes a tradition in the family, as a result causing many problems. Because the root of the matter is denial of sex in marriage, everything what a wife asks from her husband will receive a negative answer.

# In the Society

Every society has its own traditional beliefs, Mzimba is not exceptional. *Mbulu* belief is one of the many traditional beliefs followed by many people in the society of Mzimba. It has caused many problems in the society.

## Spread of HIV & AIDS

In Mzimba many people are still living a communal type of life. They build their houses close to each other. This type of living has been inherited from their ancestors. Many men who are burning with sexual passion do not walk long distances looking for women. Some of these men are those denied sex by their wives because of *mbulu* belief. Since these men cannot control themselves, they start looking for other women within the society. In this case it very difficult for this relationship to be discovered. In so doing, they easily contract HIV&AIDS, and in another way, they also spread the disease in the society. *Mbulu* belief puts many men at risk of getting HIV&AIDS in their old age. This belief of *mbulu* is endangering the society very much. Old men are getting into such problems because their wives deny them sex under the excuse of *mbulu*.

## Poor Relationships

Mzimba people live in close relationship with one another. This community in some cases turns into poor relationships because of different reasons. One of the reasons is *mbulu* belief.

> "My wife had an affair with my own elder brother. I could not understand why. I could not trust him anymore. Because of this my wife and his wife always had quarrels so I decided to shift and build my house at a distance."[35]

When it was investigated as to why this brother did this, it was discovered that he no longer sleeps with his wife because of *mbulu* belief.

Many people have wronged each other in different ways and they have forgiven each other. For example, a man stole K100,000 from his own brother. The relationship was really bitter. They could not speak to each other but after some discussion the elder brother forgave his younger brother. The life now is as usual. Although Jesus said we must forgive each other seventy-seven

---

[35] Int. Nyirenda (not real name), 20.10.2012.

times (Matt 18:22). Many men find it difficult to forgive the man who is sleeping with his wife. Because of this the relationship between the two men is always sour even if they can be brothers. One contributing factor is *mbulu* belief.

## In the Church (CCAP Synod of Livingstonia)

The church through Christ has come to liberate people from their traditions which are against the will of God. One of the beliefs is that of *mbulu*. Although many Christians have declared Jesus Christ as their Lord and Saviour, they still follow many of their traditions which brings problems in the church.

### *Losing Church Members*

There are many churches with different rules. These rules help to govern the church. This *mbulu* belief has affected some members of the church in one way or another. CCAP Synod of Livingstonia has lost many of its members in many ways. One way is through *mbulu* belief. Because of this belief, men who are still sexually active and cannot control themselves, take a second wife. According to the tradition of the church the polygamist and his second wife are suspended and are denied some of their privileges in the church. Some of the privileges which are denied to the polygamist and his second wife are: Holy Communion, baptism if he/she was not baptized, leadership and the children born from this marriage are not allowed to be baptized during their infancy as that of the first wife. Moses Mlenga has urged against this in his book titled: *Polygamy in Northern Malawi. A Christian Reassessment.*[36] This denial of privileges has caused

---

[36] Mzuzu: Mzuni Press, 2016, pp. 143-197.

many polygamists and their second wives to join other churches where they can be welcomed as full church members.

> "I was a very active church elder in CCAP but when I and my wife misunderstood each other on sexual matters because of her age, I decided to marry a second wife and join Last Church of God with my second wife, I am now a pastor."[37]

This movement to another church is due to *mbulu*. This is just one example of the many members who have left the church because of marrying a second wife due to *mbulu* belief. Even if others cannot leave the church, but the dedication someone had before suspension is quite different from the dedication after suspension. As a pastor in the church, I have seen how some people react and behave after suspension. It is a very painful situation. Some people cry when they are suspended. This is the situation the men who are suspended due to *mbulu* feel.

## Absenting themselves from Church

Some husbands are more active in the church than their wives. The opposite is true in other marriages. One of the contributing factors is *mbulu* belief. Although it is a secret between husband and wife, it has contributed to some couples to stay away from church. Some women fail to attend church because their husbands have forsaken them.

> "My husband has nothing to do with me. I am treated like a dog at home and yet he claims to be a church elder. I can't like listening to him preaching to me,"[38]

one woman lamented. Another woman complained that her husband cannot allow her to go to church. Yes, some women are

---

[37]  Int. Nyathi, pastor, Last Church (not real name), 12.12.2012.
[38]  Int. NyaMwale (not real name), 13.12.2012.

in dire poverty because the *mbulu* belief has separated them. Because of the poverty she cannot go to church. Other women are fed up with the immoralities of their husbands. They have promised to resume going to church if the practice stops. This is also true of some women; they count their husbands as nothing. This makes some husbands not to have interest in going to church. This is very common among the couples who have separated from each other because of *mbulu*. Many women who have reached this stage are very active but some are discouraged by the character of their husbands, as a result they feel ashamed to go to church. Likewise, men are discouraged by the way wives treat them at home, so going to church is like wasting their time.

## Problems in Serving God

Serving God needs peace of mind for both husbands and wives. When couples have conflicts at home, they are not fruitful at the church. Each one's eye is on watch of the other. The differences they had at home can clearly be noticed at the church e.g. how they speak to each other. The husband becomes too jealous against any man who greets his wife. The woman is not very comfortable in serving God because she has someone on her back who acts as her captain. All this is because of sexual differences at home due to *mbulu* belief.

> "This is a very big problem in our church. Some men are very watchful and jealous of their wives when they reach menopause. They feel like they are having love affairs with other men or even the parish minister."[39]

In the church many middle-aged women who have reached this stage are very active but some are discouraged by the characters of their husbands. This causes some women to have problems in

---

[39]   Int. Lovely Kamanga, Synod Women Coordinator, Mzuzu, 4.9.2012.

serving God. Likewise, some men too are discouraged by the way their wives treat them at home although these women are dedicated members of *Umanyano* (women's guild). Problems come from both sides.

# Chapter Three

# Biblical Teachings Related to *Mbulu*

One of the most important factors a Christian must understand is that sex was God's idea for man's good and man's enjoyment.[40] Here man refers to both man and woman (husband and wife). This clearly shows that sex within marriage is not a sin. Sexual intercourse is also intended by the creator as a means of expressing the love of married people for one another.[41] It is given from God to the couple which should never be denied without proper reason or agreement between husband and wife.

## Sex in the Old Testament

According to Malawian tradition, speaking about sex is a taboo. So sex issues should never be discussed in the society. But the fact that God created male and female shows that man (*munthu*) is a sexual being.

There are many texts in the OT that speak about sex. Genesis 1:31 shows that whatever God created was good, this automatically includes sex because it was also created by God. So there is no way sex is to be neglected in marriage. It was given to man (*munthu*) before the fall into sin in the Garden.[42]

---

[40] Wilbur O'Donovan, *Biblical Christianity in African Perspective*, Katunyake: 1996, p. 299.

[41] Stephen K. Msiska, *Golden Buttons: Christianity and Traditional Religion among the Tumbuka*, Zomba: Kachere, p. 49. [Reprint Mzuzu: Luviri Press, 2018].

[42] Genesis 1:28; Wilbur O'Donovan, *Biblical Christianity in African Perspective*, Katunyake, 1996, p. 299.

*Genesis 2:18:* "The Lord said, it is not good for man (*munthu*) to live alone. I will make a helper suitable for him." The emphasis here is 'suitable helper'. There can be many helpers but they might not be suitable. So in human life a suitable helper or companion (GNB) is the woman, who will provide something your close relatives such as a brother or sister, even parents cannot provide, this is sex. So denying sex to each other in marriage means marriage is incomplete according to God's plan. Although God in the Garden was a close friend of Adam, He wasn't a suitable companion.

It is not good for man to be alone. In the real sense man was not alone. He could speak with God and chat with animals but God looked at it as not good. This is the only phrase in the creation story that condemns declares something in the creation as 'not good'. God had something in mind that is hard to understand. According to Africans, failure to get married is like committing a crime against traditional beliefs and practices.[43] In this case man was incomplete, and God said that this was not good.

*"Bone of my bones and flesh of my flesh"* (Genesis 2:23). It is a deep theological word for sex in marriage. It shows the beginning but does not show the end. The two will remain bone and flesh of each other forever till death separates them.

> "Genesis 2 acknowledges that people do not find the true meaning of human life in the same mere fact of existence."[44]

If this was so, Adam would not have faced problems of loneliness because there were many animals. But a normal person finds real life in a suitable companion because human beings are sexual

---

[43]  John S. Mbiti, *Introduction to African Religion*, Second Edition, Chicago: Bridles, 1975, p. 110.

[44]  Claus Westermann, *Genesis 1-11: A Commentary*, London: SPCK, 1974, p. 226.

beings. This is very special about man; this signifies that bone can never be separated from the flesh without causing trouble or destruction. So separating a husband and wife even in the old age brings many problems in marriage, not only in sexual matters.

"The Old Testament uses flesh by itself as a term for close relationship."[45] Although in some cases the word flesh is to mean blood relations, in this verse the context is about a partner in marriage, which refers to the flesh of my flesh, not just flesh. In African tradition some words are used figuratively so that young ones should not understand the discussions of the elders, e.g. *ni munthu mulwale* (she is pregnant). In this case flesh could mean literally that, because Eve was made from Adam's side but it is also used figuratively meaning "sexual partner". So sex was ordained by God for married people. One flesh shows complete sharing with no boundaries between them. As one flesh they will constitute a new being that will endure as long as they live as Jesus confirmed in Matthew 19:6.[46]

*"The two will be united:"* this clearly indicates that the two were not completely united to their families. This unity is only complete between a husband and a wife. In marriage this unity is complete through sex. So if sex can be stopped in marriage without a proper reason or agreement between the couple, that marriage will be incomplete. Circumstances such as *mbulu* belief should not alter the loyalty and commitment of the wife to her husband.

*Proverbs 5:15-19:*

> Drink water from your own cistern,
> running water from your own well.

---

[45] Victor Hamilton, *The New International Commentary on the Old Testament: The Book Gen 1-17*, Grand Rapids: Eerdmans, 1990, p. 170.

[46] Tokunboh Adeyemo (ed), Africa *Bible Commentary: A One Volume Commentary*, Nairobi: Word Alive, 2006, p. 14.

Should your springs overflow in the streets,
your streams of water in the public squares?

Let them be yours alone,
never to be shared with strangers.

May your fountain be blessed,
and may you rejoice in the wife of your youth.

A loving doe, a graceful deer—
may her breasts satisfy you always,
may you ever be captivated by her love.

What is being described here with poetic eroticism is the beauty and blessing of lovemaking in the context of marriage.[47] Every man and woman should satisfy their sexual desires within the context of marriage. There must be no denial of sex between married couples to avoid promiscuity. Let your own wife be your source of pleasure as water refreshes a thirsty man. The wife is represented by a cistern and a well that is a continual source of fresh flowing water. This indicates that the husband should never have sex with other women apart from his own wife and vice-versa. The sexual relationship should never stop, it must be a continuous exercise as a continual source of fresh flowing water, and this water is never shared with others.

*"Rejoice in the wife of your youth."* This is a continuous action. It should never be stopped without a good reason or agreement. Indeed one can enjoy the wife or the husband through sex. This starts from the youth stage in marriage till death separates. So sex between a married couple is not a taboo in the Bible as many Africans think. It has to be practiced provided the couple is healthy. According to this passage denying sex in marriage will lead to promiscuous relationships. A man is attracted to a woman in many ways. He can be attracted just by thinking of a woman,

---

[47]   Ibid, p. 775.

by looking at her body, looking and touching her breasts, therefore wives should not always put on a bra but put it off when they are alone so that the husband can be looking at her breasts and touch them to satisfy him.

*The Song of Songs* "brings out the message that sexual desire is God given and beautiful in the context of a heterosexual, committed and loving relationship."[48] Although some scholars interpret this book allegorically, I would to interpret it literally for the benefit of those who are not theologians. According to the writer of this book, sex for a married couple is a gift from God and is to be enjoyed by both husband and wife without one monopolizing it. Many Malawian women are advised not to initiate lovemaking; if she does she will be regarded as a prostitute. "Yet the song clearly puts the female on what is at least an equal footing with the male when it comes to expression of their love."[49] In Song of Songs, it is the woman who starts to sing about her lover, while in Genesis 2:23 it was the man who starts his poetic song when God brought her to him:

> Bone of my bones
> Flesh of my flesh
> Shall be called woman
> She was taken out from me

"In this respect the Song of Songs complements the Genesis account."[50] This complement shows that husband and wife should have the same opportunity in issues of sex. Wives too have the right to ask their husbands for sex, the Bible is very clear on this opportunity in issues of sex. The Old Testament does not tell us that when a wife reaches menopause she should stop sex because

---

[48] Tokunboh Adeyemo (ed), Africa *Bible Commentary: A One Volume Commentary*, Nairobi: Word Alive, 2006,, p. 797.

[49] Ibid, p. 798.

[50] Ibid, p. 798.

she will be affected with *mbulu*. The word of God shows that sex is a continuous thing in marriage.

## Abstinence from Sex in the Old Testament

In the Old Testament there are cases when couples abstained from sex. For example; when in battle (2 Samuel 11:11); when a woman was in monthly period (Lev 18:19; 19:15; 20:18), and during some festivals and some important occasions according to the Jewish tradition.

## Sex in the New Testament

The Bible does not contradict itself since it is God speaking to his people. What is said about sex in the Old Testament is emphasized in great detail in the NT by Jesus and Paul. This shows the importance of sex in marriage.

### Matthew 19:4-6

"In marriage the husband is consecrated to the wife and the wife to the husband. The one becomes the exclusive possession of the other as much as offerings become the exclusive possession of God."[51] So when Christ said a man will leave his father and mother to cleave to his wife and they become one flesh, He meant many things, sex not excluded. Indeed sex is supremely important for married people. This is one way the married couple complement their personality. The absence of sex will narrow life in marriage. "For both partners it must bring a new fullness, a new satisfaction and a new commitment into life."[52] The above text is drawn from

---

[51]    William Barclay, *The Daily Study Bible Series: The Gospel of Matthew*, Vol 2, Revised, Philadelphia: Westminster, 1975, p. 202.

[52]    Ibid, p. 204.

Genesis 1:27 and 2:24, "which show not only that sexual union is God's creation purpose for man, but also that the union is exclusive and unbreakable."[53] One flesh is a deep expression of marriage from which sex cannot be excluded. Excluding sex in marriage is undoing God's plan of creation for marriage. "Marriage was meant to be complementary: God made them male and female"[54] This text indicates that homosexuality is against God's will of marriage, since God created male and female to complement each other. In homosexuality there is no complement. The marriage is to be a permanent relationship as indicated in the word "one flesh and be united," literally *glued*. This also explains the sexuality the couple is to enjoy. Indeed the couple is commanded to find fulfilment in each other because it is God's gift. Therefore, the *mbulu* belief should not destroy God's plan of marriage.

## 1 Corinthians 7:1-5

In the first place, before Paul starts teaching the main issue in the passage, he tries to tell the Corinthians the type of marriage initiated in the Garden of Eden. The true marriage is one wife one husband and vice versa. According to Paul in this passage, marriage has an important purpose in everyday life, "it is the remedy for fornication."[55] The heart of this passage is verse 3 in which Paul is explaining the first duty of couples to each other. One way for married people to escape lust is for husbands to have

---

[53]  R.T. France, *Tyndale New Testament Commentary: Matthew*, Leicester: IVP, 1985, p. 280.
[54]  Michael Green, *BST: The Message of Matthew*, Leicester: IVP, 2000, p. 202.
[55]  John Calvin, *Calvin's New Testament Commentaries: 1 Corinthians*, Grand Rapids: Eerdmans, 1906, p. 134.

a regular sex relationship with their wives."[56] Sex is only right between a husband and a wife not otherwise. So each couple should fulfil this duty according to the Bible. If this exercise is not fulfilled in marriage it will lead to many problems between the couple. Therefore, to avoid these complications, "married couples are to have normal sexual relationship, with the emphasis on sexual fulfilment for both the man and the woman."[57] Married couples should be free to each other on issues of sex because each has a responsibility and privilege to satisfy the other. Sex in the Bible is not a taboo but is a free gift from God.

> "Without sexual intercourse a marriage is not complete. One of the essential functions of marriage is that a man and a woman through intercourse become joined together as one body."[58]

Their bodies belong equally to one another, therefore should remain under each other's control. Not as African culture that considers the woman as the property of the husband but as Adam said, "She is bone of my bones and flesh of my flesh." This simply indicates the equality of man and woman in everything.

*"To submit to each other in marriage."* It is to accept sex to each other. Each couple should always have freedom when in need of sex. Therefore denying each other sex is totally wrong. Indeed, sexual desire is for every creature, so man is not exceptional, therefore married couples must not deprive each other. Spiritualizing marriage by either partner is not wanted in marriage. Abstinence may be there but through an agreement and for an agreed time. According to Paul, couples can abstain

---

[56] Wilbur O'Donovan, *Biblical Christianity in African Perspective*, Katunyake, 1996, p. 302.

[57] Stephen and Georgina Adei, *God's Master Plan for Marriage*, Nairobi: Word Alive, 2005, p. 121.

[58] Thomas Hale, *The Applied New Testament Commentary*, Katunyake: Kingsway, 1996, p. 421.

from sex during a time of prayer but such time must be limited. Intercourse between married partners does not defile prayers, but for proper attention they can agree to separate for a (limited) period. Couples must never deprive each other of sexual love because of spiritual affairs for it is a normal part of marriage. Paul is encouraging Christians to be in tune with each other in matters both spiritual and physical."[59] Husband and wife are in control of each other's body not only physically but also spiritually. The two should help each other in all situations because they are one body. This should be as the marriage vow indicates, *"Mu uheni na uweme, mu usambazi na mu ukavu, mu matenda na mu umoyo; kutemwana na kusanguruskana yisuke yimupatulani nyifwa."*[60] If this vow can be understood and be implemented by married couples, many problems existing in many marriages today can be reduced. "Partners deprive each other in marriage to give what God wants us to give."[61] But what is needed in marriage is equality, mutuality and to follow God's command. Indeed following God's command is to abandon some of the traditional beliefs such as *mbulu*, which are against God's will.

## *Mbulu* in the Bible?

The Bible was written many years ago. The Old Testament was written in Jewish culture and for Jewish society. The New Testament was written in a different background and for many societies during that time. In the entire Bible there is no mention of *mbulu*, although some people have misinterpreted Numbers 5:18-22 as if it is talking about *mbulu*. This passage was a test to

---

[59] Warren W. Wiersbe, *The Bible Exposition Commentary*, p.591.

[60] W.H.K. Jere (Rev. Dr.) and R.F. Ndolo (Rev.), *Ndondomeko ya Visopo*, (no place), 1986, p. 40. ("In bad and in good situations, in riches and in poverty, in diseases and in health, in love and in enjoyment until death separates.")

[61] David Prior, *BST: The Message of 1Corinthians*, Leicester: IVP, 1985, p. 116.

an unfaithful woman which would lead her to a curse if she was guilty.

> "The priest will make her drink some bitter water that will bring a curse upon her if she has been unfaithful. If she has not been involved with any other man the curse will not affect her."[62]

## Those against the *Mbulu* Belief

Although *mbulu* belief is widespread and deep rooted in Mzimba, there is a group of couples who clearly say they are not afraid of *mbulu*. These people have different backgrounds that influence them not to be afraid of the belief.

> "I am coming from a very remote area of Mzimba. This *mbulu* issue is really followed in my area. Even my own parents follow it, but I cannot tell them the truth because of tradition. In real sense this is just a belief."[63]

Christianity has come to liberate people from those traditional beliefs that are contrary to it.

> "Our norm of living is the Bible, there is no such thing as *mbulu* in the Bible, and so there is no reason to separate."[64]

Indeed, the Bible is quiet on this belief. Following this belief will mean going out of the Bible and making Christ useless. In Christianity, during marriage vows it is indicated that only death can separate the couple. The marriage vows never say be separated by *mbulu*, but only by death.

---

[62] Tokunboh Adeyemo (ed), Africa *Bible Commentary: A One Volume Commentary*, Nairobi: Word Alive, 2006, p. 177.

[63] Int. James (not real name), Clinical Officer, 2.5.2013.

[64] Int. Overtoun P. Mazunda Rev., retired minister & principal, College of Theology, Ekwendeni, 7.3.2013.

Education too has influenced many couples not to follow *mbulu* belief. Having learned in Biology and in Science how the body is created, they have a different understanding on how the body works. Because of this Biology understanding there is no fear of *mbulu* belief.

Other people in Mzimba are not afraid of *mbulu* because of their backgrounds. With intermarriages and migration of people across the country, some couples don't fear *mbulu* because it is not found in their tradition. This is because *mbulu* belief is mostly followed in Mzimba. So people from other districts living in Mzimba don't follow the tradition but follow the tradition of their origin. To them *mbulu* belief has nothing to do with their life style.

> "There is no such thing as *mbulu* in Karonga. I can't follow it just because I live in Mzimba. I can follow some Ngoni beliefs which are helpful to me but not this one."[65]

Some Ngoni have copied from other tribes of the country not to be afraid of *mbulu*. The young generation too has another understanding of the 21st first century which clearly says there is no *mbulu*.

---

[65] Int. Mwangomba, Kafukule, 26.1.2013.

# Chapter Four: Pastoral Advice

> "Sex is not just a tiresome exercise as some think. It is a necessity in marriage. It plays a very important role in the union between husband and wife."[66]

If there is lack of sex in marriage, the marriage is incomplete and this may lead to many problems. But if it is used accordingly the couple will enjoy and it will invigorate the marriage. One way of satisfying each other in marriage is through sex because it is the gift given by God to couples to show love to each other.

> "In married life we are happy only as far as we give happiness and the sex act will only be successful if it implies the gift of oneself."[67]

Sex, if not used accordingly, will bring bitterness in marriage. If one of the couple seeks his or her own pleasure, it will be one sided and therefore incomplete

## Advice to Newly Married Couples

In Ephesians 5:25 Paul says, "Husbands, love your wives just as Christ loved the church and gave himself up for her." This is very important for a married man although hard to implement in many cultures. But this is a command from God to a married man.

> Such divine love goes far beyond sexual love or even friendship love. It sacrifices itself for the one it loves.

When the wife looks at the husband, she should picture Christ at work in him. This great caring love will automatically make a wife to submit to her husband. In this case *mbulu* cannot separate the

---

[66] Gaston Deluz, *A Companion to 1 Corinthians*, London: Longman, 1963, p. 80.

[67] Ibid, p. 82.

two partners. But this love is lacking in many husbands because of following different cultures. They don't love their wives. "He just enjoys using my body to satisfy himself." Indeed many husbands don't love their wives but only their bodies. In so doing marriage becomes incomplete. "Husbands should show great patience and gentleness with their wives, especially in their sexual relationship." In Ephesians 5:22-23, Paul instructs Christian wives to submit themselves to their husbands as to the Lord. "What Paul is saying is that wives are to honour, respect, and serve their husbands as an act of obedience to God himself." If love and obedience between husband and wife work hand in hand, marriage is enjoyable. This is what Christian marriage should be. Christian marriages should not be rooted in traditional beliefs such as *mbulu*. It should never be one sided. Un-biblical traditions such as *mbulu* should not be followed in marriage to avoid complications. This shows that love should be the centre of every Christian marriage. Any belief such as *mbulu* weakens marriage.

## Advice to Modern People

Every person is brought up in a particular culture. In a real sense no culture is perfect for all people. The modern person is influenced by many things, just to mention a few: science and technology, the present context, his/her own culture, other people's culture etc. Because of these influences, many marriages have lost their direction. Each spouse is doing his/her own way and as a result, the purpose of marriage is lost. But for Christians, the standard of married life is the Bible. Every belief must be followed in reference to the Bible and in line with the time we are living. Any belief contrary to the word of God is not relevant. The Holy Spirit is still at work revealing to the modern man the truth about the word of God. People must be attentive to the Holy Spirit and must interpret the Bible as lead by the Spirit. When Christ came he was not against culture but the transformer of culture.

He transformed what was against the will of the Father. For this reason the Pharisees and the teachers of the Law hated him. He is ready even today to transform our own culture. *Mbulu* belief, although deep rooted in Mzimba, Jesus is ready to transform it for the betterment of married couples to enjoy sex, not only *mbulu* belief, but also other beliefs which are contrary to the word of God. While the modern man is influenced by time he/she must be careful not to miss the track and disobey God because of the new understanding of things. While modern people believe that some cultures are good and this modern life is good too, they must always do the will of God within their cultures and in this modern world to enjoy their marriage. The Bible is silent on this belief, this shows it is not relevant for Christians to follow. If some people followed it or are following, they are doing this in ignorance. Jesus himself taught on marriage, and so did Paul, but they never mentioned about it, so this belief is manmade and therefore against the will of God.

## Advice to Traditionalists

Traditionalists are the custodians of the traditional beliefs. To them changing their belief will bring some consequences from their forefathers. They have been following these beliefs all along. They don't mind whether the beliefs are meaningful or not. Change of time has nothing to do to their lives. But as time passes, everything changes. For instant, the way of living, languages, understanding of things are not as they were 50 years ago. Some of the beliefs were very meaningful some decades ago but cannot be meaningful today. Traditionalists should understand these changes.

> "When I was young I was not allowed to eat eggs. I was told that eggs cause diseases in children and in women. I believed and

followed the instruction. But when I grew up I discovered that it
was not true."[68]

Indeed this belief of children and women not eating eggs was real
in Mzimba and some people still follow it in some areas today. In
the same way, *mbulu* belief has been followed by many women in
Mzimba but there is no truth in it. Although it was followed in the
past it cannot be followed today because the understanding of
people has changed. Traditionalists should find the truth of the
beliefs they follow since they just inherited them from their
parents. Finding the real truth about a particular belief is
important. Find out, do not just follow it. Many beliefs are
followed in many parts of the country just because our ancestors
followed them, though they are not helpful in our day to day
living. As time changes, the understanding of people changes too.
Beliefs should be practiced for the benefit of all people in that
particular society and for the glory of God.

## Advice in Marriage Seminars

Many couples have different understandings about their
marriages. For some the source of marriage is tradition. In such
cultures a person who has passed the age of marriage and yet is
not married is not regarded important in the society. Because of
this marriage is cultural.

> "When a girl is sought in marriage she undergoes a further period
> of instructions whereby she is given detailed advice in respect of
> the mysteries of womanhood, wifeship and mothercraft."[69]

These instructions corrupt the understanding of marriage. For
others marriage has its root in the Bible, but they misunderstand

---

[68]   Int. Watson Chisambi, retired teacher and elder, CCAP, Kafukule, 26.1.2013.
[69]   Dolb S. Mwakanandi, "The Role of African Traditional Religion in the Promotion of the Christian Life," PhD, University of Stellenbosch, 1990, p. 57.

why God instituted marriage. Because of this, marriage is interpreted in different ways to different people according to their understanding of the Bible. God instituted marriage for many reasons, but because of time and space I will only mention two which are of importance in this book. Firstly, God created marriage for fellowship. In Genesis 2:18, God said, "It is not good for man (*munthu*) to be alone." God was there and animals were there but could not provide this fellowship to the man. The fellowship God is speaking of in this text is very unique because it is between man and woman. Because of this uniqueness, husband and wife should never be separated by anything. Therefore *mbulu* cannot separate this fellowship because God ordained it. The second reason God instituted marriage is for sexual satisfaction. In Genesis 2:24-25 God said,

> "For this reason a man will leave his father and mother and be united to his wife, and they will become one flesh. The man and the woman were both naked and they felt no shame."

This unity is very special in God's eyes. It is the unity of the flesh. Separating the flesh will lead to destruction. The nakedness without shame is only between married couples. In reality this refers to sex. Therefore *mbulu* belief cannot separate the couple. If *mbulu* belief is followed today, it means that the fellowship God intended is no longer there, which will be against the will of God. Also sexual satisfaction which God intended will no more be in existence. During creation God never gave limitations on sex for a couple. Even today the Bible speaks to us the same thing. Therefore a couple should never stop sex because of *mbulu*, as the Bible is against such behaviour.

While some traditional beliefs are good, some are the opposite. Those which are relevant for our living and are in line with the word of God must be encouraged. But those which are not good and are not relevant for our day to day living and are not in line with the word of God must be discouraged completely, because they will only bring problems. Since we are new creatures in Christ, the old must be abandoned for the sake of Christ. Christians should never have trust in the living dead. Having the belief in the ancestors will make Christ useless. Christians, Christ must always remain our Lord and Saviour. Since the Bible is silent and biology has proved its non-existence, there is no *mbulu*.

> "This is just a belief. Even young ladies who have not reached menopause are found with swelling in their womb. Swelling in the womb is just a disease. It has nothing to do with sex in old age,"

said Mama Chavula, a retired nurse. Because of this, *mbulu* is not an issue in many other cultures, and married couples enjoy sex through all their years.

# Bibliography

## *Published Sources*

Adei, Stephen and Georgina, *God's Master Plan for Marriage*, Nairobi: Word Alive, 2005.

Adeyemo, Tokunboh (ed), *Africa Bible Commentary: A One Volume Commentary*, Nairobi: Word Alive, 2006.

Barclay, William, *The Daily Study Bible Series: The Gospel of Matthew*, Vol 2, Revised, Philadelphia: Westminster, 1975.

Calvin, John, *Calvin's New Testament Commentaries: 1 Corinthians*, Grand Rapids: Eerdmans, 1906.

Deluz, Gaston, *A Companion to 1 Corinthians*, London: Longman, 1963.

France, R.T., *Tyndale New Testament Commentary: Matthew*, Leicester: IVP, 1985.

Green, Michael, *BST: The Message of Matthew*, Leicester: IVP, 2000.

Hale, Thomas, *The Applied New Testament Commentary*, Katunyake: Kingsway, 1996.

Hamilton, Victor, *The New International Commentary on the Old Testament: The Book Gen 1-17*, Grand Rapids: Eerdmans, 1990.

Harawa-Katumbi, Chimwemwe, The Interaction between Christianity and Traditional Medicine in the Livingstonia Synod, MA, University of *Malawi*, 2003.

Jere, W.H.K. (Rev. Dr.) and R.F. Ndolo (Rev.), *Ndondomeko ya Visopo*, (no place), 1986.

Mbiti, John, *Introduction to African Religion*, Second Edition, Chicago: Bridles, 1975.

Msiska, Stephen K., *Golden Buttons: Christianity and Traditional Religion among the Tumbuka*, Zomba: Kachere, p. 49. [Reprint Mzuzu: Luviri Press, 2018].

Mwakanandi, Dolb S., "The Role of African Traditional Religion in the Promotion of the Christian Life," PhD, University of Stellenbosch, 1990.

O'Donovan, Wilbur, *Biblical Christianity in African Perspective*, Katunyake, 1996.

Prior, David, *BST: The Message of 1 Corinthians*, Leicester: IVP, 1985.

Westermann, Claus, *Genesis 1-11: A Commentary*, London: SPCK, 1974.

Wiersbe, Warren W., *The Bible Exposition Commentary*, Victor Books, 1989.

*World Book 2001, Volume 13*, Chicago: World Book Inc.

# Oral Sources

Int. Maggie Soko, (not real name) church elder, CCAP, 6.1.2013.

Int. Nyasulu, church elder, CCAP, (not real name), 26.1.1013.

Int. Adams retired teacher and church elder, CCAP, (not real name), 26.1.20213

Int. Chavula, Ekwendeni, 12.2.2013.

Int. Gogo Mfipa, (not real name), 12.2.2012.

Int. Nyauhango, (not real name) 12.9.2012.

Int. NyaGondwe (not real name), 19.9.2012.

Int. Gogo Nyausowoya, (not real name), 26.1.2013.

Int. NyaMwale, (not real name), 2.9.2013.

Int. NyaNkhambule, (not real name), 19.9.2013.

Int. Eunice Phiri, Women Coordinator, Njuyu Presbytery, 9.9.2012.

Int. Mhango, retired teacher, (not real name), 24.112012.

Int. NyaMoyo, (not real name), 26.11.2012.

Int. Nkhoswe, (not real name), 26.2.2013.

Int. Mary Mhango, Nurse, Enukweni Health Centre.

Int. Mrs Kawelama, Matron, Ekwendeni Mission hospital, 2.1.2013.

Int. Mwale, (not real name), 6.9.2012.

Int. NyaBanda, (not real name), 6.9.2012.

Int. Zakeyo, (not real name), 6.9.2012.

Int. Saka, (not real name) 22.10.2012.

Int. Soko, (not real name), 19.10.2012.

Int. James, Clinical Officer, (not real name), 2.5.2013.

Int. Overtoun P. Mazunda, retired minister and Principal, College of Theology, Ekwendeni, 7.3.2013.

Int. Agness Thawi, Women Coordinator, Ekwendeni Presbytery, 3.9.2012.

Int. Nyirenda, (not real name) 20.10.2012.

Int. Nyatha, pastor of Last Church, (not real name), 12.12.2012.

Int. Lovely Kamanga, CCAP, Synod Women Coordinator, Mzuzu, 4.9.2012.

Int. Watson Chisambi, retired teacher and church elder, CCAP, Kafukule.

Int. Mwangomba, Kafukule, 26.1.2013.

Printed in the United States
By Bookmasters